Pizza Making

20 Homemade Pizza Recipes

Table of Contents

Introduction

Being an Italian dish, Pizza holds a great significance in the history of food industry. Although the initial form of pizza only contained flat baked bread with the simple topping of tomato sauce and cheese, but with the passage of time, pizza has passed through the different stages of revolution. The latest form of pizza is so yummy and mouth-watering that one can't help but grab a slice of pizza and thrust it into his/her mouth. Pizza has turned into a universal food. It doesn't matter whether you belong to a European country or an Asian country, pizza is for everyone.

Pizza is loved by people belonging to every age group. Whether you are a two year old toddler or a 90 year old woman, pizza is the favorite dish of every person. When it comes to the advent of pizza, the common answer is that pizza originated from Italy. The very first chapter of this book will provide you with the valuable information on the origin of pizza and how pizza passed through the different stages to reach its most modern form. You will also get to know about the most desirable pizza toppings in this book.

Some of the people think that making a pizza is a very time consuming act which in fact is not true. If you want to learn how to make pizza in just a few minutes then easy-to-make recipes in the second chapter of this book are going to amaze you with every word you read.

Italian pizzas are the most famous and traditional pizzas around the world. Various chefs belonging to other countries try to imitate the recipe of an Italian pizza so they can amaze the world with their expertise in pizza making. The part of this book containing the top pizza recipes of Italian history will guide you how to create Italian master pieces in your kitchen. The fourth and fifth chapters of this book will provide a complete guidance regarding the unique and healthy recipes for pizza.

Chapter 1 – The History of Pizza Making

Common perception is that pizza basically originated from the Italy, which is in fact true. The delicious word of Pizza was derived from the Latin word of "Pinsa". Pinsa basically means flat bread.

If we ponder over the history of this marvelous dish then we will come upon an amazing legend about the origin of the pizza. This legend states that during their stay in the Palestine held by roman, the roman soldieries fell deeply in love with the local dish by the name of "Jewish Matzoth". When these soldiers went back to their homeland they tried to develop a dish of similar taste and nature.

Later on the archeologists found a pizza belonging to the Bronze Age in the preserved form, from the Veneto region. During the tenure of middle ages, people witnessed a more modern approach in the preparation of a pizza. Pizza was a favorite dish among the peasants of that time. They prepared it with whatever they could access, whether its herbs or spices, vegetables or meat. Pizza-making attained the level of an art by those simple peasants.

Pizza gained a completely different shape when later-on the use of Mozzarella cheese became common in Pizza. Mozzarella cheese or mozzarella di buffalo became very common after the Italians discovered about the Indian Water Buffalo. The taste of Mozzarella cheese is so unique and out-of-this world that no other cheese can take the place of this mouth-watering cheese. Although there are many traditional pizza recipes that require the use of other kinds of cheeses but every time a different cheese is used in the pizza, it is used in combination with the mozzarella cheese.

Most of the people these days, love the taste and aroma of tomato sauce in the topping of pizza. But you will be amazed to know that before the arrival of 18th century, there wasn't a sign of tomato sauce in the Italian pizza. Although tomatoes were present in the Italian markets since 1530's, but most of the people thought them to be poisonous so never used them in their cuisines. But again the peasants changed the mind of all the other classes of Italy. They used the tomatoes as a test in the pizza topping and the results were just amazing. Tomato sauce became a mandatory part of the Italian pizza since the 18th century due to its intoxicating taste.

The initial form of pizza was introduced by the peasants belonging to the Naples but later on the popularity of this Italian dish increased so much that even the people from upper class showed interest in adopting it as their regular food item. The vendors, who used to sell pizza on the streets of Italy, opened their own pizza outlets that were visited by people wishing to eat pizza with different and unique toppings. You can ask for what kind of toppings are those sellers offering and then you can go for the one which cherishes you the most.

The first ever pizza restaurant of Italy celebrated its inauguration in 1830 and from then on the pizzas prepared by this restaurant are unbeatable.

Types of Pizza

Although Pizza is termed as the national dish of Italy, still there are many other countries that offer the most delicious types of pizza.

When it comes to the American pizza, there are two common types of pizzas available in different states of America.

- Chicago-styled pizza-this type of American pizza contains thick crust and heavy cheese.

- New York pizza-this type of American pizza is thin and contains traditional tastes.

Even the Italian pizza-makers offer two different types of pizzas.

- Italian Pizzas

- Pizzas belonging to different cultures of the world

Some of the most famous types of pizza include:

- Margherita

- Lahma Bi Ajeen

- Stromboli

- Calzone

- Neapolitan

- Marinara

- Deep Dish

Except for these different types of pizzas, most of the countries of the world have their own traditional types of pizzas.

Most wanted Pizza Toppings

Some of the most wanted pizza toppings of the world include:

- Pepperoni

- Bacon

- Cheese

- Sausage

- Pineapple

- Ham

- Chicken

- Onions

- Mushrooms

- Green pepper

- Olives

- Shrimp

- BBQ sauce

- Red peppers

- Hamburger meat

- Tomato

- Jalapeno

- Garlic

- Salami

- Canadian Bacon

These toppings play the role of great taste-triggers whether applied individually or in blend with each other.

Chapter 2 – Easy-To-Make Pizza Recipes

Before jumping right the pizza recipes, we must first know how to make pizza dough. The first two recipes in this chapter will tell you how to make pizza dough in the quickest possible way. You should try these recipes given in this book to enjoy the variety of taste offered by these pizzas.

Easy-to-make pizza dough recipes

Recipe no-1. Pizza Crust (Classic)
Ingredients

- Warm water.................................one cup

- Dry yeast(active)..........................one packet

- Cooking oil.................................one tablespoon

- Sifter flour.................................two and a half cups

- Salt..one teaspoon

Method

First take a mixing bowl of a large size and then add flour and yeast in it. Also add the salt in the above mentioned amount. Mix all three items. Now you must add the one cup water but in a gradual manner. After adding the water, mix it a little and then add oil. Next comes the beating which must be done at the low speed. After three seconds, you must again mix the mixture properly and try to take off the extra material attached to the sides of the bowl and again start beating. This time you will be beating in a high speed motion.

You must stop the beating after three minutes. Now you have add a little stiffness to the dough and for this purpose, you must add further flour but in a balanced amount. After adding the further flour, you must try to blend it with your hands and start kneading. You must keep on kneading for at least 10 to 15 minutes until you feel that the dough seems a little soft and smooth. Now take a bowl and grease it from the inside. Place the dough inside that bowl and turn it over several times so it gets greasy from every corner.

You must then let the dough sit for at least 90 minutes after covering it so the dough can increase in the size. You must again knead it a little bit to push it back into the bowl and then put it in the fridge for at least two hours. After the passage of two hours, you must take it out and then cut it with a knife in two equal halves. Add some flour on the surface and then smooth out both of these halves keeping the thickness level of 1/8 inch and the circumference of around 12 inch.

You must add yummy toppings after you have brushed a bit of oil on the dough surface. The pizza must be baked for almost 25 minutes at the temperature of 425 degree.

Recipe no-2. Boboli Crust for Pizza
Ingredients

- Water...................................one-fourth cup

- Salt.......................................one teaspoon

- Warm water.......................21/4 cups

- Flour...................................six cups

- Yeast(dried).........................one package

- Olive oil..............................six table spoons (you must also keep a little extra amount for oiling the pans.)

Method

First of all we need to prepare yeast by dissolving it into water carrying the temperature of 105 degrees. Let the yeast rest in the water for two to three minutes. Now you must all put other items into the yeast. After mixing them for a while, you must take the mixture out from the bowl and place it on the kneading board and start kneading. You must keep on kneading for at least 10 minutes. After you have done with kneading, put the dough in the bowl and give it around 40 to 45 minutes to rise. Don't forget to cover it with wet towel or a cotton cloth.

You must cut the dough in two to three parts according to its quantity. Take three pie pans. Oil them with olive oil and then settle the three parts of dough in them. You must make slight holes in the crust with the help of your finger tips. Make a mixture of the following herbs and then place it on the top of the dough.

- Rosemary (chopped)

- Kosher salt

- Thyme

- Ground pepper (fresh)

Dough will take at least one hour to rise and then you must bake the dough at 350 degrees. After 25 minutes, the pizza crust will be ready.

Recipe no-3. Simple Pizza Dough

Ingredients

- Warm water ....1 1/3 cups

- Flour..3 ¾ cups

- Salt...1 ½ tsps

- Yeast..1 packet

- Sugar..1 table spoon

- Olive oil...................................three tablespoon (keep a little extra amount of olive oil for brushing)

Method

If you want to make pizza in the quickest way possible then this recipe is perfect for you. All you need to do is to thrust the flour into a bowl and then add salt in the flour. Make some space in the flour with your fist and then add warm water in it. Do mix it gradually while adding the water. After adding water, you must add yeast and sugar into the mixture and blend it further with your hands.

Add the olive oil when the dough gets a thick and foamy look. After this you must start kneading the dough for at least five to seven minutes. After you are done with kneading, take some olive oil and apply it on the top of the dough with the help of a brush. Now you must let the dough sit for at least 90 minutes after covering the bowl. Once it has gained the double mass, divide it into two equal halves of around one pound.

Quick and easy pizza recipes

Recipe no-4. New York Pizza

Ingredients

- Olive oil...................................one cup
- Mozzarella cheese.................two cups
- Tomato sauce......................half cup
- Oregano (dried)................for garnishing
- Pecorino.........................for garnishing

Method

Oil the pizza pan. Place the dough in the pizza pan. Spray some olive oil on the top and then spread tomato sauce on the surface of the dough.

Sprinkle mozzarella cheese on the top. After baking, decorate the pizza with garnishing ingredients.

Chapter 3 – Recipes for Italian Pizza

Whether they are good or bad, Italian pizzas are known as the world's best pizzas.

Well there isn't any doubt in it because "Pizza" basically originated from Italy. So if you really want to taste true pizza then you must try these yummy-licious Italian pizza recipes at home. They are very tasty and above all, they are easy to make.

Recipe no-5. Italian Cheeseburger Pizza

Ingredients

- Chopped onion.................1 (small sized)

- Pizza crust.....................12 inches (in the ready-to-eat form)

- Pizza sauce...................8 ounces

- Bacon strips..................6 (must be cooked)

- Beef................half pound (minced or grounded)

- Mozzarella cheese..........8 ounces

- Italian seasoning............1 tsp

- Cheddar cheese.............8 ounces

- Pickle slices(dill)...........20

Method

Thrust beef and onions in a frying pan and cook them for around half an hour. Do check the meat's condition after every five or seven minutes. When the meat seems tender and has changed color then you must drain it and let it cool down.

Now first oil the pizza pan and settle the crust in it. For the topping, you must apply the pizza sauce all over the surface of the crust. Now pour the curry of beef on the curst surface. Try to sprinkle this curry in an even way on every part of the crust. Sprinkle the cheese, and then decorate with pieces of bacon. Adjust the pickle pieces on the top and then spray a little of the Italian seasoning. Let it bake for at least 9-10 minutes at the temperature of 450 degree.

Recipe no-6. Pizza with garlic and spinach topping

Ingredients

- Olive oil..................one tbsp

- Garlic.........................minced

- Pizza crust.................pre-baked (12 inches diameter)

- Chopped spinach.....10 ounces (must be frozen and properly drained)

- Mozzarella cheese......one cup (in shredded form)

- Tomatoes....................2 small sized (thin slices)

- Feta cheese.............four ounces(preferably containing herbs and garlic)

- Rosemary...............one teaspoon

- Parmesan cheese......one pack (grated)

Method

Take a microwave bowl and add garlic and olive oil in it. Mix them. Set the microwave to HIGH and turn it on for half a minute. Brush the pizza pan with oil and settle pizza in it. Now apply the topping on the surface.

Adjust the cheeses, spinach and slices of tomato on the top of the crust in a beautiful manner. At the end sprinkle the herbs on the top and then bake for ten minutes at the temperature of 450 degrees.

Recipe no-7. Taco Themed-Pizza

Ingredients

- Beef...................one pound (Grounded)

- Taco seasoning.....................one envelop

- Pizza crust.........................pre-baked(12 inches diameter)

- Water.............................one cup

- Salsa.............................3/4th cup

- Refried beans....................16 ounces

- Cheddar cheese................8 ounces (shredded)

- Tortilla chips.................two cups (crushed)

- Tomatoes.......................two small sized (chopped)

- Lettuce...........................1 cup (shredded)

Method

Add beef in a saucepan and cook until it changes color and becomes tender. Drain the beef. Add water and then add taco seasoning. Mix. When the mixture starts to boil, lower the heat under the pan. Remove the cover from the pan. After the mixture has simmered for 10 to 12 minutes, remove the pan from the stove and let it cool down.

Settle the crust in the pizza pan and then start adding the topping. Add the salsa, chips, beans, cheese, and the beef curry on the top and adjust them in an attractive way. Let the pizza bake for 10 to 15 minutes at the temperature of 350 degrees.

Recipe no-8. Pizza on Pita bread

Ingredients

- Pita bread..........................one

- Pizza sauce.........................2 tbsp

- Mozzarella cheese................1/4 cup

- Oregano

- Garlic powder

- Basil

- Olive oil

Method

Apply olive oil on the pita bread with the help of brush.

Now spread sauce, and shredded cheese on the bread. Add the spices and desired topping. Let the bread bake for at least 7-10 minutes at the temperature of 400 degrees.

Recipe no-9. Pesto Pizza with chicken topping

Ingredients

- Dry yeast......................................2 tsps(must be dry and active)

- Warm water..............................1 cup(heated at 110 degree)

- Sugar...one tbsp

- Salt.......................................one and a half teaspoons (in separate portions)

- Bread flour..............................2 and ¾ cups

- Olive oil................................two tsps and one tbsp (in divided portions)

- Chicken breasts.....................half a pound (Skinless, must be in small pieces)

- Onion.................................small size, sliced

- Green pepper.........................1/2

- Red pepper.........................1/2

- Yellow pepper...................1/2

- Mushrooms....................half cup (fresh, in slices)

- Pesto.............................three tbsp (prepared)

- Mozzarella cheese..............6 ounces (shredded)

- Pepper............................1/4 tsp

Method

Take a large sized bowl, add yeast in the bowl and then blend it with water. Now add the flour one cup, oil one tbsp, salt one tsp and sugar. Mix and beat these ingredients for a while and then add the further flour and beat again.

Start kneading for at least 6 to 8 minutes, stop when the mixture becomes smooth. Take a bowl and brush it with cooking oil. Place the mixture in it and then turn the mixture up-side down so the entire mixture gets coated with the oil. Now cover the bowl and put it on the side. After one hour the mixture might have raised to the double mass.

Take a frying pan. Add chicken, peppers, oil, onion, and mushrooms in the frying pan and cook them until the chicken changes its color. Move away from the stove.

Now place the dough in the pizza pan and add the toppings. First you must spread the pesto over the dough and then you must add the chicken mixture topping. Next you must add the cheese on the top. At the end, you must add salt and pepper on the dough.

Now put the pizza in the oven and bake for at least 20-25 minutes at the temperature of 400 degrees.

Chapter 4 – Recipes for Breakfast Pizza

Having a breakfast equipped with nutritious items is very important for the health and well-being of our body. Breakfast is an important meal of the day so it must contain the food items equipped with all the necessary nutrients. Eating nutritious food items for breakfast doesn't mean that you must have heavy and fattening breakfast. It means you must eat breakfast that keeps you healthy and happy. Although preparing pizza at the breakfast time might seem a little complicated but these quicky pizza recipes are going to help you surprise your kids with a delicious pizza each day.

Recipe no-10. Pizza with Meatballs

Ingredients

- Pizza crust..pre-baked (with 15 inches diameter)

- Olive oil...................................one cup

- Tomato sauce..........................half bowl

- Mozzarella cheese...................seven to eight ounces

- Meat balls.................................sliced after cooking

- Basil

- Pecorino

Method

Oil the pizza pan. Settle the pre-baked pizza crust in the pan. Start the topping by spreading the tomato sauce on the top surface. Scatter the pieces of mozzarella cheese and put in the oven for baking. When the pizza seems crispy, take it out and decorate it with meat balls. You must also add the olive oil, sprinkle with the herbs and then bake till the pizza gets brown.

Recipe n0-11. Sicilian Pizza

Ingredients

- Dough

- Tomato sauce....................................3/4 cup

- Mozzarella cheese..............................two cups (in shredded form)

- Olive oil...one cup

Method

Take a baking sheet and apply oil on it with the help of a brush. Place the dough on this sheet and press it. Let the dough rest for a while after covering it. When it has increased in mass, apply the toppings. First spread the tomato sauce on the dough surface. Sprinkle the mozzarella cheese. Spray drops of the olive oil. Bake it until it becomes brown and crispy.

Recipe no-12. Pepperoni Pizza

Ingredients

- Dough

- Tomato sauce..................................$3/4^{th}$ cup

- Mozzarella cheese..........................one and a half cup (in shredded form)

- Olive oil..one cup

- Pepperoni.....................................6 ounces (must be in sliced form)

- Bocconcini..................................4 ounces

- Pecorino.....................................for garnishing

- Basil..for garnishing

Method

Apply oil on the baking sheet. Prepare the dough. Place the dough on the baking sheet and let it increase in mass. Spread the tomato sauce on the dough. Add the cheese in scattered form. Sprinkle the olive oil over and around the dough. Bake until the dough changes color and seems crispy. Now add the topping of bocconcini. Also add the above mentioned amount of pepperoni.

Bake into the oven until you see bubbles appearing on the surface of the dough. Sprinkle the herbs.

Recipe no-13. Herb Pizza

Ingredients

- Dough

- Olive oil......................half cup

- Salt..............................to taste

- Oregano

- Thyme.........................(in chopped form)

Method

Smooth out the dough in to a round-shape with the help of bread-roller. Apply the olive oil on the top and spread it evenly on the surface. Further sprinkle the pizza dough with oregano and salt.

Also add the thyme on the top. Keep on baking until the dough turns golden-brown and looks crispy. Apply the olive oil in the end.

Recipe no-14. Pizza with Smoked Mozzarella

Ingredients

- Dough
- Olive oil....................................one cup
- Salt...to taste
- Thyme...................................... (in chopped form)
- Oregano

- Garlic clove...........................one (in minced form)

- Smoked mozzarella...............six ounces (in sliced form)

- Ricotta...................................3/4 cup

- Parmesan...............................(in grated form)

Method

First prepare the pizza like the Herb pizza. When you have finished the topping of herbs, add the garlic, and smoked mozzarella on the top. Let the pizza bake until it changes color and becomes golden crispy.

Sprinkle the Parmesan on the top and also add the ricotta. Let it bake until the topping starts to melt on the surface.

Recipe no-15. Zucchini Pizza

Ingredients

- Dough
- Garlic................................(in minced form)
- Zucchini...........................(in slices)
- Olive oil...........................half cup
- Red pepper

Method

First of all, you must stretch the dough with the bread-roller into a rectangular form. Apply the topping of the zucchini and other items mentioned in the ingredients list. Let the pizza bake until it changes color and gains the crispy look.

Recipe no-16. Tomato based pizza with bacon topping

Ingredients

- Olive oil...................................half cup
- Onions.....................................2 cups (in sliced form)
- Salt...to taste
- Pepper....................................to taste
- Pita breads..........................4 (must be according to the Greek style)
- Brown sugar.......................three tbsp
- Mozzarella cheese.............half a cup
- Garlic powder...................add according to the taste
- Tomatoes.........................two (in sliced form)

- Spinach..........................one and a half cup (not compulsory)

- Bacon............................eight slices (in ready-to-eat form)

- Asiago cheese..............one cup(in shredded form)

Method

Set the oven temperature at 400 degrees. Turn on the stove to the medium heat. Next you need to take olive oil one tbsp and heat it over the stove in a frying pan. Next you must add the onions in this oil. Sprinkle the onions with the salt. Stir and later on add the pepper on it. Cook the onions for at least four to five minutes. When the onions turn tender, add the brown sugar. Cook on till the color of the onions change to light brown. Take off the frying pan from the stove and let it cool.

Now you must take a baking sheet and coat it with few drops of olive oil. Spread the oil with the brush. Settle the pieces of pita bread on the baking sheet. Again apply the olive oil on these pieces with the help of brush. Scatter the breads with mozzarella cheese after scattering the garlic powder on them. Now you must first arrange the layer of onions and then the layer of tomatoes on these bread pieces. Only add the spinach if you like the taste of it, otherwise you can ignore it. Top the bread pieces with pieces of bacon that are cooked.

Let the pita bread pieces bake for at least 10 minutes so the topping can get tender. Take the bread pieces out of the oven. Add the remaining cheese. Place them back and take out after a few minutes when you see the cheese melting on them.

Chapter 5 – Recipes for Healthy Pizza

Recipe no-17 .Eggplant pizza with parmesan topping

Ingredients

- Marinara sauce..................................3/4 cup

- Dough...(must have been refrigerated)

- Mozzarella cheese........................two and a half ounces(must be skimmed or half-skimmed)

- Tomatoes....................................three(small sized)

- Ricotta cheese...........................half cup (must be skimmed)

- Parmesan cheese.....................one tsp (must be in grated form)

- Basil

- Eggplant................................3/4 pounds(must be in sliced form)

Method

Apply the oil to the pizza pan. Place the dough on the pan and then start applying the topping. First you must apply the marinara sauce on the pizza dough.

Now scatter the mozzarella cheese, ricotta cheese, eggplant and tomatoes on the top. Before baking add the parmesan as a final topping ingredient. Bake for almost 10 to 15 minutes at the temperature of 450 degrees. Add the basil before serving.

Recipe no-18. Greek Pizza

Ingredients

- Dough...(must be refrigerated for a couple of hours)

- Oregano....................................one tbsp (must be in chopped form)

- Marinara sauce.........................half a cup

- Grape tomatoes..........................one cup (cut into the halves and softened through broiling)

- Feta...half cup

- Onions.......................................half a cup (must be cooked and diced into small pieces)

- Shrimp......................................8 ounces (medium sized)

Method

Place the dough in to the pizza pan. Apply the marinara sauce as the base for the topping. Place the rest of the ingredients on the top of the dough after applying the sauce. Bake for at least 10 to 15 minutes at the temperature of 450 degrees. Before serving scatter the oregano on the top.

Recipe no-19. Potato Pizza

Ingredients

- Dough.......................................(must be refrigerated for a couple of hours)

- Fontina cheese..........................3/4 cup (in shredded form)

- Rosemary.................................1 tsp (finely chopped)

- Potatoes...................................half pound

- Rosemary.................................1 tsp (chopped)

- Bacon slices.............................four (must be cooked)

- Parmesan cheese....................one tbsp (grated)

Method

First you must place the dough in the pizza pan after applying the oil inside the pan. Cover the dough with the fontina cheese. Scatter the rosemary on it that has been in the finely chopped form.

Now you must add the potato slices on the top of it. After that, add the topping of bacon and chopped rosemary. At the end scatter the parmesan cheese. Now you must let it bake for at least 10 to 12 minutes at the temperature of 450 degree.

Recipe no-20. Fennel-Taleggio pizza

Ingredients

- Dough

- Olive oil......................half cup

- Salt...............................to taste

- Oregano

- Thyme...........................(in chopped form)

- Fennel....................(must be sautéed)

- Taleggio................6 ounces(must be in slices)

- Pecorino..................(must be grated)

- Hazelnuts.................2tbsp(must be chopped)

Method

Take dough and make roll it out smoothly with the help of bread-roller. Spread the olive oil on the top of the dough. Also add the salt and the other herbs on the top. Put it into the oven and let it bake till it changes the color. When it turns golden-crispy, take it out and again spread some drops of olive oil on the top. Now add the topping of fennel and hazelnuts. Also add the pecorino and taleggio on the top and put it again into the oven for a few minutes. Take it out when the topping starts to melt. Another healthy pizza is ready.

Conclusion

Most of the people love to eat pizza but they are unable to do so because of the heavy and fattening nature of the pizza. This book is for all such people who have been living on tasteless diet food due to their sickness. The chapter of healthy pizza recipes is a miracle for all such people. Not only are these recipes easy-to-prepare, but they are extremely healthy, and yummy recipes. Whether you are suffering from any disease or trying to maintain your body weight, these low-calories and highly nutritious pizza recipes are excellent for you.

As mentioned before, pizza is not just a sort of fast food item but it is much more than that. After reading the recipes in this book, you might have understood that pizza-making is not less than an art. After reading the first chapter of this book, you might be feeling amazed at the legendary history of this mouth-watering dish. Well who would have thought that pizza was originally invented by the peasants? Due to its rich nature and unique blend of ingredients, it seemed like the food of upper class people.

Most of the mothers love to show their love by making special dishes for their kids and relatives. This book is not just a recipe book but it is a pathway for you to reveal your love to your family members by the incredible art of pizza making.

A bundle of thanks to you for spending your time in downloading and reading this book. I hope this book brings a positive change to your life.

FREE Bonus Reminder

If you have not grabbed it yet, please go ahead and download your Free Ebook *"Dump Dinners Crock Pot: 31 Surprising And Delicious Recipes For Your Crock Pot And Slow Cooker For Each Day of Month!"* Simply Click the Button Below

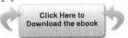

OR **Go to This Page**
http://easycookingideas.com/free

BONUS #2: More Free Books
Do you want to receive more Free Books?
We have a mailing list where we send out our new Books when they go free on Kindle. Click on the link below to sign up for Free Book Promotions.
=> Sign Up for Free Book Promotions <=

OR Go to this URL
http://bit.ly/1WBb1Ek

Made in the USA
Lexington, KY
09 December 2018